Contents

Democracy and the News Media

"Nothing could be more irrational than to give the people power and to withhold from them information, without which power is abused. A people who mean to be their own governors must arm themselves with the power which knowledge gives. A popular government without popular information or the means of acquiring it is but a prologue to a farce or a tragedy, or perhaps both."

James Madison

Democracy can be an effective form of government only to the extent that the public (that rules it in theory) is well-informed about national and international events and can think independently and critically about those events. If the vast majority of citizens do not recognize bias in their nation's news; if they cannot detect ideology, slant, and spin, if they cannot recognize propaganda when exposed to it, they cannot reasonably determine what media messages have to be supplemented, counter-balanced, or thrown out entirely.

On the one hand, world-wide news sources are increasingly sophisticated in media logic (the art of "persuading" and manipulating large masses of people). This enables them to create an aura of objectivity and "truthfulness" in the news stories they construct. On the other hand, only a small minority of citizens are skilled in recognizing bias and propaganda in the news disseminated in their country. Only a relatively few are able to detect one-sided portrayals of events or seek out alternative sources of information and opinion to compare to those of their mainstream news media. At present, the overwhelming majority of people in the world, untrained in critical thinking, are at the mercy of the news media in their own country. Their view of the world, which countries they identify as friends and which as enemies, is determined largely by those media (and the traditional beliefs and conventions of their society).

This slanted information is not a "plot" or a "conspiracy." It is simply a matter of educational background and economic reality. Journalists and news editors are themselves members of a culture (German, French, Mexican, Chinese, Korean, Japanese, Indonesian, Russian, Algerian, Nigerian, North American, etc.). They share a view of the world with their target audience. They share a nationalized sense of history and allegiance, often a religion, and a general belief-system. An Arab editor sees the world different from an Israeli one. A Pakistani editor sees the world different from an Indian one. A Chinese editor sees the world different from an

American one. The same is true of news reporters and other journalists.

What is more, news people work under severe time restrictions (in constructing their stories) and limitations of space (in laying out or presenting their stories). It is hardly surprising that profound differences are reflected in news coverage from nation to nation and culture to culture.

In any case, only those who understand the conditions under which world media operate have a chance of controlling the influence of their national media upon them. Our goal in this publication is to help our readers lay a foundation for transforming the influence of the media on their lives. It is in all of our interests to critically assess, rather than mindlessly accept, news media pronouncements. Our hope is that we can aid readers to become more independent, insightful, and critical in responding to the content of news media messages and stories.

Myths That Obscure
the Logic of the News Media

The media foster a set of myths regarding how they function. Believing these myths impedes one's ability to view the news from a critical perspective. They include the following:

- that most news stories are produced through independent investigative journalism

- that news writers simply report facts in their stories and do not come to conclusions about them

- that fact and opinion are clearly separated in constructing the news

- that there is an objective reality (the actual "news") that is simply "reported" or described by the news media of the world (our news media writers reporting on this objectively; the media of foreign enemies systematically slanting and distorting it)

- that what is unusual (novel, odd, bizarre) is news; what is usual is not

Bias and Objectivity in the News Media

The logic of constructing news stories is parallel to the logic of writing history. In both cases, for events covered, there is *both* a massive background of facts *and* a highly restricted amount of space to devote to those facts. The result in both cases is the same: 99.99999% of the "facts" are never mentioned at all (see Figure 1).

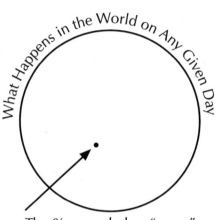

The % recorded as "news"

Figure 1
What Happens in the World on Any Given Day

If objectivity or fairness in the construction of news stories is thought of as equivalent to presenting all the facts and only the facts ("All the news that's fit to print"), objectivity and fairness is an illusion. No human knows more than a small percentage of the facts and it is not possible to present all the facts (even if one did know them). It isn't even possible to present all the *important* facts, for many criteria compete for determining what is "important." We must therefore always ask, "What has been left out of this article?" "What would I think if different facts had been highlighted here?" "What if this article had been written by those who hold a point of view opposite to the one embedded in the story as told?"

For example, people commonly consider facts to be important to the extent that they have significant implications for them personally: Is any given event going to affect what they want, how much is it going to cost them, how is it going to influence their income, their living conditions, their leisure, their convenience? How some given event is going to affect others, especially others far away and out of sight, is quite another matter. There is therefore a large divergence among the news media of the world as to what is presented as "significant" in the world.

The media focus on what their readers personally care about. Thus, even if their readers are irrational in some belief (e.g., harbor some irrational hate). The media nevertheless will treat that hatred as rational. Hence, when slavery was commonly accepted in the United States, the media presented slavery as "natural." When the country became divided on the issue, the media followed suit (each paper presenting as right what its readers believed to be right).

> "Most people, having given up on getting a set of unadorned facts, align themselves with whichever spin outlet seems comfortable."
>
> *The Wall Street Journal*
> May 7, 2004

Consider how news media treat what is "shocking" or "exciting" or "disgusting" or "delightful" to a social group. For example, a woman sun-bathing on a beach with bare breasts is commonplace on the French Riviera (therefore is not condemned and her behavior is not treated as "news") but the same woman would be arrested and punished for sun-bathing in a similar way at a beach in Lebanon (therefore would be condemned and her behavior treated as "news"). Or again, during the Olympics each country's news media focus their attention on those events in which their nation's athletes are expected to do well. And when one of their athletes wins a gold metal in an event, this event is presented to the home audience as if it were much more important than the events in which they won no metals. National audiences often are "thrilled" by "their victories" and uninterested in victories of others.

Human "objectivity" is an ideal that no one perfectly achieves. It requires a great deal of intellectual humility (knowledge of our extensive ignorance) and begins by freely admitting one's own point of view, as well as the need to consider competing sources of information and opinion when making important judgments.

The key point is this: There are (typically) *multiple* points of view from which any set of events can be viewed and interpreted. Openness to a range of insights from multiple points of view and a willingness to question one's own point of view are crucial to "objectivity." This can be suggested in a diagram that illustrates how multiple viewpoints often stand in relation to the same set of events (Figure #2). Objectivity is achieved to the extent that one has studied a wide range of perspectives relevant to an issue, obtained insights from all of them, seen weaknesses and partiality in each, and integrated what one has learned into a more comprehensive, many-sided whole. Each should serve to "correct" exaggerations or distortions in the others and to add facts not highlighted in the others.

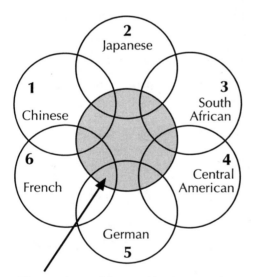

- Only some of the facts are highlighted in any point of view
- All points of view ignore or play down some facts
- No one point of view provides total understanding
- Understanding multiple viewpoints increases insight

The total set of facts relevant to understanding a given set of events

Figure 2
Six Points of View Focused on the Same Set of Events

We gain in "objectivity" (in conceptualizing both history and the news) to the extent that we can put stories and narratives into a rich historical context, and comment on them from multiple points of view. For example, to understand the war between Britain and its colonies in North America (1776–1783), one must look at the events from at least three points of view: that of the British government, that of the Colonial leaders, and that of the indigenous peoples.

> "The media world we inhabit is without exception a world of 'spin'"
>
> *The Wall Street Journal*
> May 7, 2004

To achieve objectivity, we need to: identify the point of view from which a given news story or historical account is constructed, identify the audience it is written for, recognize what points of view it is negating or ignoring, and distinguish the raw facts behind the story from the interpretation and spin being put on those facts. When we do this, we are not as easily manipulated.

We are able to exercise greater independence of judgment. We get a greater sense of what elements of the story or account are most credible and which are the least. Of course, it is hard to do any of these if we have not also discovered multiple sources for information and a way to determine when those sources are most credible.

> "Newspapers tend to signal the importance of an article or image by the prominence of its placement..."
>
> *The New York Times International*
> May 11, 2004

Forms of Objectivity

"Objectivity" may appear in three ways. Two are genuine. One is a façade, a counterfeit of objectivity.

The Objectivity of Intellectual Humility. The first form of objectivity is based on the possibility of developing intellectual humility, knowledge of our ignorance. Thus, a critical consumer of the news knows the difference between hearing a story and verifying the truth of that story. A critical consumer of the news knows that what is presented as fact in the news may not be fact. It may be propaganda, misinformation, distortion, or half-truth. Knowing this, critical consumers of the news "bracket" what they hear, read, and see in the news. Recognizing that they don't themselves know the facts, they "suspend" belief. They take in information in a tentative fashion ("This may or may not be true!"). For example, "objective" jurors will not come to a conclusion of guilt or innocence after hearing only one side's case. Unfortunately, intellectual humility is a rare quality in human life. The majority of people in the world have been exposed to a limited range of views and have been most influenced by the viewpoint dominant in their own culture. As a result, they take themselves to be in possession of the TRUTH. This confidence is in fact proof of their lack of objectivity. They do not know what intellectual humility is, and they do not take steps to achieve it.

The Objectivity of Fair-minded, Multi-dimensional Thinking. A second form of objectivity goes beyond the first. It is based on intellectual humility and also on having done substantial intellectual work in reasoning within multiple conflicting points of view in addressing questions, problems, and issues of significance. It is connected to positive insight into the complexity and many-sidedness of most important world issues and large-scale conflicts. Those who have achieved this state can insightfully role-play multiple perspectives on a multitude of issues. They can identify and weigh relative strengths and weaknesses within those perspectives. They are comfortable playing the role of dissenter, though they don't dissent for the sake of dissent. They reject party lines, sociocentric mind-sets, and intellectual conformity. They are intellectually independent, are intellectually perseverant, and have intellectual integrity.

Sophistic Objectivity. The third form of objectivity is "sophistic." This intellectual state results from studying a range of views with the overriding motivation to defend a predetermined choice. This mind-set is common in intellectuals who make their income (and achieve their prestige) as apologists for powerful interests. The temptation to become an apologist for a well-established point of view or economic interest is enormous because money, position, and prestige are involved. Lawyers and politicians, as well as public relations experts, are typically ready to play such a role. Most national news commentators routinely play such a role. They present positions consistent with a picture of the world shared by most of their readers or viewers. They are viewed by their audience as "objective" only to the extent that what they present reflects mainstream views.

> "How many photos of naked Iraqis does one want to see?"
>
> Col. Allan, editor in chief, *New York Post*, May 10, 2004

The Perception of Bias in the Mainstream

Quite naturally, but uncritically, people think of those who agree with them as objective and those who disagree with them as biased. Thus, if news commentators present mainstream views with a liberal spin, they are viewed as "objective" only by the liberals in the audience. If mainstream views are given a conservative spin, they are viewed as "objective" only by the conservatives in their audience. The media therefore present liberal or conservative slants on the news in accordance with their audience's views.

Propaganda and News Story Writing

Webster's New World Dictionary defines propaganda as *"any systematic, widespread dissemination or promotion of particular ideas, doctrines, practices, etc. to further one's own cause or to damage an opposing one."* Given this definition, there is no clear-cut dividing line between news story writing

> "What is on the front page is more difficult to avoid than what is inside."
>
> *The New York Times International* May 11, 2004

with a given cultural audience in mind, on the one hand, and constructing propaganda on the other hand. Both systematically play down or seek to minimize the worth of opposing perspectives or points of view. The logical similarity is striking. Even historical writing can take on the character of propaganda when it is written to "glorify" or "demonize" certain groups of people by suppressing or ignoring information that does not support its preconceptions and favored ideology.

Because the word "propaganda" carries with it a negative connotation (suggesting deception or distortion), few news writers would admit that the word applies to their stories. Yet the fact remains that if one receives most of one's news from a single cultural or national source, the likely impact on the mind will be that of distortion and deception. Most people, as a result, are trapped in one world view (because they have received a steady diet of stories and accounts articulated from that perspective and have not seriously considered any alternatives).

"...because of the nudity and humiliation on display in the Iraq photographs, many newspapers have chosen to put articles about them on the front page, but the images inside."

The New York Times International
May 11, 2004

This does not mean, of course, that a given world view is unvaried. Not everyone who shares a viewpoint agrees on every issue. Not every German agrees with every other German, yet a significant difference exists between those who see the world from a German perspective and those who see it from, say, a Japanese or a Mexican perspective. What is more, though virtually every point of view carries some insight, it doesn't follow that there is *equal* insight in all of them.

It is usually much easier for people to recognize the truth of these tendencies when thinking about the news coverage in other nations or cultures—especially when those other nations and cultures differ greatly from their own. Israelis easily recognize bias and propaganda in Arab coverage though they see little in their own coverage, and vice versa.

When President George W. Bush of the United States gave a speech identifying Iran, Iraq, and North Korea as an "axis of evil," his speech was favorably received by the majority of Americans. It was taken as a follow-up of the President's promise to "rid the world of evil." A wave of patriotic fervor was sweeping the nation. The national news media had engendered a communal sense of rage. For the overwhelming majority of Americans, the American government stands for high ideals (liberty, justice, democracy, free enterprise, human rights). The President defending the country against its enemies with the might of its armed forces is an image inspiring patriotic emotions.

The speech, however, was not received in the same way abroad. He was roundly condemned by the news media in Iran, Iraq, and North Korea and was also viewed as arrogant and out of touch with the complexities of reality by "allies" of the United States. Here are some of the ways the French and German media conceptualized the speech to their national audiences:[1]

- "In France, the afternoon daily *Le Monde* ran a front-page cartoon of Mr. Bush in battle fatigues and a headline saying, 'Mr. Bush points out his latest enemies.'"

- "A television editorialist on LCI, France's 24–hour news station, said the speech belonged to 'a sheriff convinced of his right to regulate the planet and impose punishment as he sees fit.'"

- "In Germany, an editorial in the daily *Suddeutsche Zeitung* offered Chancellor Gerhard Schroder sympathy as he heads for Washington tonight. "'Poor Gerhard Schroder,' the editorial says. 'It can't be easy being the first grumpy European to appear at the throne of the freshly anointed American Caesar.'"

Here is a sense of the news media coverage in Iran and North Korea:

- Iran: "Bush intends to divert public opinion from the Middle East issue and to prepare the domestic grounds for continuing his support of Israel in its brutal oppression of the Palestinian nation." (Iran state radio report)

- "North Korea's official media scoffed at Mr. Bush for identifying the nation as among the world's most dangerous. It said his 'loudmouthed threat' was intended to justify an American military presence in South Korea."

---

[1] All above quotes were taken from the *New York Times*, January 31, 2002, p. A12

Of course, in virtually every case it is easier to persuade people that "foreign" press coverage is biased than to persuade those same people of their own national press bias. Every nation's press coverage of the "news" appears to the mass public of that culture as expressing self-evident truth — because the news is routinely presented within the world view of the mass public that "consumes" that news.

When trapped in a culture-bound view of the world, one thinks within a web of self-serving assumptions, thinking that it is others (our national or cultural enemies and opponents) who use propaganda and manipulation while we, being honest and just, always give the other side its due. Others use propaganda and manipulation. We freely express the truth. This mind-set is not the product of a conspiracy or intrigue. It is the natural and predictable outcome of national news media attempting to make a profit by presenting events in the world to a home audience.

Protecting the Home Audience from Guilt Feelings

The events for which news coverage is most taboo in mainstream media news are deeds that indict the home culture or society of ethical wrong-doing. Consider, for example, the extent of civilian suffering following the dropping of atom bombs on the cities of Hiroshima and Nagasaki by the United States military. Though some debate has taken place in the United States media on these acts, to our knowledge the United States mainstream media have presented little documentation of the enormous suffering caused by those events.

One might compare, for example, documentation of the suffering of civilians in German extermination camps (which has been and continues to be extensive) with that of the Japanese populations of Hiroshima and Nagasaki when subjected to massive atomic radiation. Scanning the fifty years since the event, we found only one article in one American newspaper, the Santa Rosa *Press Democrat* (in Northern

California) documenting in detail the suffering of the civilian population. The article was a guest editorial by David R. Ford, who worked in
1965 for a CBS television affiliate in Honolulu and is presently living in
the Santa Rosa, California, area. Here are excerpts (without the horrific details) from his editorial:

"In 1965... I spent a vacation in Hiroshima, Japan. My purpose: To
interview the sick and dying 20 years after the atomic bomb was
exploded over that city on Aug. 6, 1944... I began the visit in the
women's ward." [What follows in the article are detailed images of
suffering that American readers would
find extremely painful to imagine their
government as inflicting (200,000 civilians
died in Hiroshima alone on that day.)] The
American reporter said to a Japanese vic-
tim, "'But we dropped millions of pamphlets warning citizens to evacuate the
cities.' He looked into my eyes. 'No paper
was ever dropped. No warning was ever
given.'"

> "We are certainly
> not going to let
> images with nudity
> or gore or violence
> go on the air."
>
> John Banner, executive producer
> of ABC's *World News Tonight*

We cannot, of course, attest to the truth
or falsity of the allegation of the U.S. fail-
ure to forewarn the civilian population.
For our purposes, the significance is the almost complete absence of
documentation of how the citizens of Hiroshima and Nagasaki suf-
fered at the time and in the 50 years following the events. Given our
analysis, the absence of documentation of these events by the
American media is exactly what we would predict from a national
mass news media. People do not pay for news that leads them to
question the "goodness" of their own nation or makes them feel
responsible for the large-scale suffering of others. They pay to see the
events of the world in a way that validates their values and alle-
giances.

Fostering Sociocentric Thinking

The key insight is this. The major media and press in *all countries of the world* present events to the world in terms that presuppose or imply the "correctness" of the ideology (or ideologies) dominant in the country. Our hope is not in changing the news media. News reporters and editors operate within a system of economic imperatives and constraints that dominate their work. Their audience is captive to an enculturated conception of the world.

As aspiring critical consumers of the mass media, we must learn to recognize that mainstream news is inevitably based on a sociocentric view of the world. We must learn how to recognize national and cultural bias. There is no reason to suppose that the ideology dominant in our culture is more accurate or insightful than that of any other. Supposing that one's own culture is exceptionally truthful in presenting its picture of the world is evidence not of insight but rather of ethnocentrism. Sociocentrism is a fundamental characteristic of all countries and cultures. The news media function as unwitting agents of social conventions and taboos.

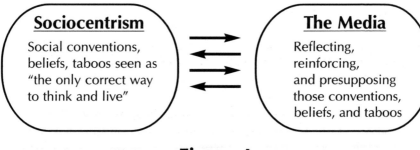

Sociocentrism

Social conventions, beliefs, taboos seen as "the only correct way to think and live"

The Media

Reflecting, reinforcing, and presupposing those conventions, beliefs, and taboos

Figure 4
A Mutually Reinforcing Relationship

Many examples of sociocentric thinking can be found in the mass media. The media are an inherent part of the culture within which they function. And remember, those in the media must "sell" their stories. Their papers, news broadcasts, and magazines must be economically successful to remain in business:

> "Pressure to increase the profits of media companies has not been an isolated phenomenon. Throughout the American economy, there is unprecedented pressure to maximize profits, putting shareholder value ahead of all other considerations. The corporations that own the news media are subject to all the business trends and economic demands that have reshaped American business in the 1980s and 1990s, affecting nearly every part of society."[2]

Because much of the thinking within any given culture is sociocentric in nature to begin with, the news media have little choice but to package what they produce within a sociocentric framework. The vehicles of large-scale social communication within a society inevitably serve that society and advance its self-image. Biased coverage is the rule, not the exception.

The mainstream news media around the world are thus biased toward their country's "allies," and prejudiced against their "enemies." They therefore present events occurring in the countries of their allies in as favorable a light as possible, highlighting their "positive" deeds while downplaying their negative ones. When generating news stories about their "enemies," the opposite treatment inevitably follows. Generating positive stories about the admirable characteristics of one's enemies is unacceptable. At the same time, negative stories about enemies are always popular, routinely generated and highlighted. The ability of a news consumer to identify these biased stories in action and mentally "re-write" them with an opposing bias is a crucial critical thinking skill. With it, one sees slanted constructs everywhere in the news. And when one sees through the bias, its persuasive effect on the mind disappears.

---

[2] *The News About the News*, by L. Downie and R. Kaiser (New York: Knopf, 2002), p. 25.

Slanting Stories to Favor Privileged Views

Every journalist knows intuitively which terms to use when characterizing the favored and unfavored players on the world stage (as pictured within a cultural perspective). We *plan*...They *plot*. We are *clever*...They are *sneaky*. We form *strategies*...They *conspire*. We have *convictions*...They are *fanatics*. We are *proud*...They are *arrogant*. We *stand tall*...They *brag* and *bluster*. We build weapons to *defend* ourselves...They build weapons to *threaten* us. We *intervene*...They *invade*. We have *religious convictions*...They are *fanatics*. We are *freedom-fighters*...They are *terrorists*. We violate treaties when they are *obsolete*...They violate treaties because they are *irresponsible, untrustworthy, and unethical*.

Journalists routinely select words that reinforce the prevailing views among the readership or audience for whom they are writing. Ironically, if news persons writing for a mainstream audience were to adopt views that significantly diverged from those dominant in their society and presented the news in accordance with those views, they would be considered "biased" and "irresponsible." If you think in accordance with mainstream views, you are a "responsible" thinker; if not, you are "irresponsible."

The exception occurs, of course, if significant numbers of people in the culture hold conflicting views, as in the conflict between liberal and conservative perspectives (expressed differently in most cultures). In this case, both points of view are presented in both favorable and unfavorable terms (depending upon whether the source is dominated by conservatives or liberals). Nevertheless, if one's views do not fall into either the mainstream liberal or conservative purview, one is dismissed as a "radical." Radicals are irresponsible by definition (as they do not agree with one of the two traditional views).

The following newspaper excerpts exemplify how the news media across the world do not objectively report the news, but cater to the views of their readers.

   1. **Source: *Press Democrat*, March 26, 2003. "Foreign Media Shows Different Iraq War Than U.S. Outlets."**

"Journalists from around the world are reporting the war in Iraq through a very different lens than U.S.-based media, one often colored by a mistrust of the Bush administration and U.S. intentions in general. 'You see a lot more skepticism in other parts of the world,' said Alice Chasan, editor of *World Press Review*, which compiles reports from media in other countries. The context of many foreign reports is 'What is the United States really trying to do? Is the war necessary?' she said "Whatever happens is being seen through the prism of President Bush being 'arrogant.' By contrast, 'among the U.S. press there tends to be a bandwagon effect and a fog of patriotism that has at times appalled me,' Chasan said. 'It's something you don't see elsewhere.'... 'I think that most American journalists have been remarkably uncritical in covering the war,' said Tom Buk-Swienty, U.S. bureau chief for the Danish *Weekendavisen*. 'In an effort not to look unpatriotic and in order to please the majority of people in this country, some parts of the press have almost become a PR machine instead of being a watchdog that one would expect in a democracy,' he said. Patriotic displays include a U.S. flag adorning one corner of the front page of the *New York Post*. Meanwhile, broadcast reporters 'embedded' with U.S. units in the region have begun to use the personal pronoun 'we.' U.S. based outlets have agonized over matters of taste as they weigh their audiences' appetite for gruesome photos."

2. **Source: *Press Democrat*, April 4, 2003. "The War Americans Don't See," (editorial by Rami G. Khouri, executive editor of the *Daily Star*, a Beirut newspaper).**

"The Arab press — like Arab public opinion as a whole — predominantly opposes the British and American attack on Iraq, and does not hesitate to say so in its front page headlines, articles and photographs. Yet the press is neither monolithic nor uniformly anti-American. ...Samples... from front pages this week in the Arabic language (and in Algeria's case, French-language) press demonstrate the United States and the Arab world do see a different war unfolding. But the front pages of leading newspapers in and around the Arab world include both American and Iraqi perspectives and feature dramatic photographs that show United States forces as both aggressors and humanitarians. One recent front page photo showed an Iraqi civilian pouring tea for an American soldier. More common, though, are images of dead and maimed Iraqi children, parents wailing over the coffins of relatives killed by American bombings, extensive damage of Iraqi civilian buildings and Iraqi civilians being humiliated by American and British troops. Sometimes, an image that would get an innocuous description in an American newspaper is given a more sinister interpretation in the Arab press. Coverage tends to mirror ideology. The quality regional press like *Asharq al Awsat* and *Al Hayat*, edited in London and printed through-out the Middle East, are the most balanced. More ideological papers with narrow readerships reflect the sentiments of their financial backers and tend to cater to the nationalistic, political and emotional views of their audiences. The tone of opinion columns and editorials is heavily anti-American. Only occasionally do Arab writers like Ghassan Tueni in Beirut's *AN Nahar*, call for the end of Saddam Hussein and his regime (and that is coupled with a rejection of American occupation)..."

Commentary: This editorial supports the thesis that the press in every country presents events in the world as confirming what their audience (and the backers of their newspaper) already believe. Not only is this thesis borne out at a national level, but at a regional level as well. Hence, the *Press Democrat* (published in a liberal area of California) carries this editorial, which argues that the Arab press is not entirely biased against the U.S. It's title emphasizes the

need for Americans to broaden their sources of information ("The War
Americans Don't See"). In contrast, the *New York Times*, in reporting on the
Arab press strongly suggests that it is biased against the U.S. and Israel, while
the U.S. press, we are tacitly led to believe, is objective, balanced, and fair. See
the next excerpt.

**3. Source: *New York Times*, April 4, 2003. "Arab Media Portray War as
Killing Field."**

"It was a picture of Arab grief and rage. A teen-aged boy glared from the rubble of a
bombed building as a veiled woman shrieked over the prostrate body of a relative. In fact,
it was two pictures: one from the American-led war in Iraq and the other from the
Palestinian territories, blended into one image this week on the Web site of the popular
Saudi daily newspaper *Al Watan*. The meaning would be clear to any Arab reader: what is
happening in Iraq is part of one continuous brutal assault by America and its allies on
defenseless Arabs, wherever they are. As the Iraq war moved into its third week, the media
in the region have increasingly fused images and enemies from this and other conflicts into
a single bloodstained tableau of Arab grievance. The Israeli flag is superimposed on the
American flag. The Crusades and the 13th century Mongul sack of Baghdad, recalled as
barbarian attacks on Arab civilization, are used as synonyms for the American-led invasion
of Iraq. Horrific vignettes of the helpless — armless children, crushed babies, stunned
mothers — cascade into Arab living rooms from the front pages of newspapers and television screens…the daily message to the public from much of the media is that American
troops are callous killers, that only resistance to the United States can redeem Arab pride
and the Iraqis are fighting a pan — Arab battle for self respect… The rage against the
United States is fed by this steady diet of close-up color photographs and television footage
of dead and wounded Iraqis, invariably described as victims of American bombs. In recent
days, more and more Arabic newspapers have run headlines bluntly accusing soldiers of
deliberately killing civilians. Even for those accustomed to seeing such images from Arab
coverage of the Palestinian-Israeli conflict, the daily barrage of war coverage in newspapers
and on hourly television reports has left many Arabs beside themselves with anger. 'He is
"Shaytan," that Bush,' shouted Ali Mammouda, a newsstand operator in Cairo, using the
Arabic word for Satan and pointing with shaking hands to a color photograph in one of his
newspapers. The image, published in many Arabic papers, showed the bloody bodies of a
stick-thin woman and a baby said to be victims of American shelling in central Iraq. They
were lying in an open wooden coffin, the baby's green pacifier still in its mouth. 'Your
Bush says he is coming to make them free, but look at this lady,' Mr. Hammouda
exclaimed. 'Is she free? What did she do? What did her baby do?'"

Commentary: This article implies that there is no truth in the Arab media's
coverage of civilian casualties in the Iraq war. The *New York Times* readership
is basically conservative, overwhelmingly supporting both the Israeli government and the U.S.-led invasion of Iraq. The readership is therefore primed to
reject any coverage of the war that negatively portrays U.S. forces, the U.S.
government, or the Israeli government. Since the article heavily criticizes the
Arab media's coverage of the Iraq war, the story is not "buried," rather it is
given a prime place in the paper (front page).

How to Obtain Useful Information from Propaganda and Standard News Stories

Obtaining useful information, even from propaganda and one-sided news stories, is possible but only if one learns to read, hear, or view them critically. This means that we must analyze the stories with a clear awareness of the point of view they embody, recognizing the attempt to influence our thinking and beliefs. One must analyze them as one analyzes one side of a multi-sided argument. One-sided presentations are not the truth pure and simple, though they contain at least part of the truth, the part that supports the side in question. What is more, in standard news stories something of the opposing point of view is often mentioned (though, usually, in fine print, deemphasized in the last few paragraphs of the story, or couched in terms or quote marks, suggesting that the reader should dismiss it).

Critical readers recognize one-sidedness and seek out viewpoints that are dismissed or ignored. They also note which stories are highlighted (e.g., on the front page) and which are buried in the background (e.g., on page 24). Here are some key questions we should ask when analyzing and interpreting news stories:

- What is the intended audience?

- What point of view is being privileged?

- What point(s) of view is (are) being dismissed or played down?

- How can I gain access to the point of view being negated (from those who most intelligently understand it)?

- Which stories are featured on the front page and why?

- What information is "buried" in the article and why?

Steps in Becoming
a Critical Consumer of the "News"

1) Understand the basic agenda of "news story construction":
Always keep in mind that the ultimate purpose of mainstream
"news story fabrication" is to sell "stories" for a profit to particular audiences (each with particular beliefs, values, and prejudices).
It is not to educate. It is not to be fair to all sides (all sides are
rarely represented in the target audience). To sell news stories to
an audience, one must carefully construct those stories in such a
way as to engage intended readers, and reinforce or validate their
beliefs, values, prejudices, and world view. Journalists typically
come from those who share the beliefs, values, prejudices, and
world view of the intended audience. The "slanting" of the story is
then achieved "naturally."

Constructing news stories for an audience requires that one determine:

a) what the audience would consider a "story" (what they would,
   and would not, be interested in),

b) what about a story would be considered most relevant and
   what about it would be considered least relevant to the audience (therefore, what to play up and what to downplay),

c) how to construct "leads" or "headlines" for a story (to create an
   initial definition for the reader),

d) how much space or time to give a particular story,

e) how to relate the story to other stories and to the audience's
   picture of themselves and their world, and

f) how to tell the story so it sounds "professional" (objective and
   unbiased to the readers, a mere accounting of bare facts).

**2) Use one's knowledge of the logic of "news story construc-
tion," first, to "deconstruct" stories in the news and then to
"reconstruct" them imaginatively with alternative biases and
slants.** One becomes a critical consumer of the news media, first,
by understanding the agenda of the news media, the criteria the
news media use in constructing the news (deciding what a "story"

is, what stories to cover, how to cover them to get the highest ratings or sell the most newspapers or magazines). Skilled consumers of the news learn how to identify and assess national, social, and political emphases and agendas. They learn how to read between the lines and how to imaginatively recast **stories-as-told** into alternative **stories-as-they-might-have-been-told** from other points of view.

3) **Learn how to redefine issues, access alternative sources (both within and outside the mainstream), put events into a historical perspective, notice and assess assumptions and implications.** Systematic questioning and assessment are crucial to the critical processing of media messages.

4) **Learn how to identify low-credibility stories by noticing vested interests or passion associated with content.** Stories are least credible when the interests of the producer or receiver of a story are involved or when the passions of a mass audience are involved (mass fear, anger, hatred, patriotism, etc.). When a nation is at war, for example, stories about the war told by the nation's press (including all explanations of it) are suspect, as all nations produce mass propaganda during war to build support for it. Stories about persons involved in taboo sexual acts (approved in other societies) would be another such a case, because the "disgust" experienced by the reader would command telling the story in such a way as to justify that "disgust" as a reasonable response ("Nudists Arrested," "Sexual Predator Condemned"). Stories that arouse mass passions are typically highly one-sided in nature and thus should have low credibility to those who think critically.

Media Awareness of Media Bias

To what extent are the news media aware of bias and propaganda in their own constructions? This question does not have a definitive answer. All journalists are aware that they are writing for an audience. It does not follow, however, that they have thought through the implications of this. Certainly, some journalists are much more aware than others.

In the United States, Israel is a favored "ally," so mistreatment or abuse of the Palestinians by the Israelis is usually covered under the idea of "justified reprisal." Because Fidel Castro of Cuba is viewed within the United States as an enemy, mainstream news writers routinely present Castro and Cuba in a negative light, ignoring or explaining away any "achievements" of the Cuban government (such as universal medical coverage and a low infant mortality rate). If and when persons in the news media recognize patterns of news coverage such as these, they must be careful in writing about them—lest they themselves be labeled "irresponsible" and "biased."

Sensitivity to Advertisers

Every group within a culture is not equally important to the news media. National media are, of course, biased in favor of national culture, religion, dominant beliefs, and social values. But within any complex culture, some groups play a more powerful role than others within media logic. For example, much news media profit comes from advertisers. These advertisers are not pleased if they, or the interests they represent, are cast in a bad light by the media they finance. News media, therefore, avoid generating stories that negatively feature major advertisers. Put another way, because news media outlets can select from among a large mass of potential stories, and cannot, in any case, carry more than a small percentage of what is available, they naturally, all other things being equal, choose to avoid or play down stories irritating to their advertisers. There are, of course, exceptions to this pattern. A lot depends on the "splash" the story would make or whether it is already "out."

Sensitivity to Government

National news media are always sensitive to the power of government. For one, national governments typically license and regulate news media by law. For another, much national news is "given" to news media through high governmental officials and agencies. For these reasons, news media personnel hesitate to criticize the national government in certain fundamental ways. For example, if the national government names some other group or nation as an enemy, the national news media generally present the "enemy" as unfavorably as they can. If the government attacks another nation militarily, the national news media line up like cheerleaders at a sporting event. The news media are typically apologists for the policies and acts of the national government.

An exception to this occurs when elements in the national news media are linked to a political party not presently in power. Their protection then comes from the power and interests represented by the opposition party. They then are beholden to the views and beliefs of their political supporters. In the United States, particular news outlets are sometimes more influenced by the Democrat or Republican parties, but both parties unite around the same basic world view and beliefs of the broader society. Both identify the same countries as friends or enemies; both are responsive to major economic forces and concentrations of wealth and power.

The basic logic is always the same. The media are presenting the news within a point of view. The point of view represents interests affecting media profitability and deeply entrenched in social ideology. The news media always focus on profit, though that focus is obscured and kept in the background.

> "The national television networks have trimmed
> their reporting staffs and closed foreign reporting
> bureaus to cut their owners' costs. They have tried
> to attract viewers by diluting their expensive news-
> casts with lifestyle, celebrity, and entertainment
> features, and by filling their low-budget, high-prof-
> it, prime-time "newsmagazines" with sensational
> sex, crime, and court stories."[3]

---

[3] *The News About the News*, by L. Downie and R. Kaiser (New York: Knopf, 2002), p.10.

Sensitivity to Powerful Interests

News media sources try to maximize their profit while minimizing costs. Investigative journalism is more expensive than pre-packaged stories (news from press releases, news conferences, and speeches). Realizing that their position of power within the culture is threatened if they fail to maintain a favorable public image, powerful economic interests continually invest in marketing their image to the public. There is therefore a symbiotic relationship between powerful media sources (which need news stories) and powerful economic interests (which generate and disseminate news stories in their interest). This is true in virtually all nations.

Powerful industries such as manufacturing, communications, agriculture, weapons producers, airlines, the criminal justice industry (prisons, police, lawyers, social workers, prison contractors), construction, banking, auto, insurance, public relations and advertising, broadcasting, entertainment — all are involved in shaping the daily news in their interest. Governmental agencies and persons in positions of power in the executive, legislative, judicial, military, and intelligence communities are all involved in shaping the daily news in their interest. Religious groups, professional groups, unions, and other groups organize around vested interests and invest heavily in shaping the daily news in their interest.

> "From the Great Depression in the 1930s through World War II and the beginning of the Cold War in the 1950s, reporters seemed to reflect establishment views more often than they exposed the failings and foibles of the powerful. They seldom challenged government news management or the press agentry of private business and the entertainment industry."[4]

Because most people's fundamental source of information about the world comes through the mass media, favorable news media coverage is a significant variable in achieving a favorable public image.

---

[4] *The News About the News*, by L. Downie and R. Kaiser (New York: Knopf, 2002), p.19.

Sensitivity to Their Competitors

News media provide the news in light of the news other media out-lets focus on. When some of the major outlets treat a story as "big," the others typically pick it up so as not to be viewed as deficient in coverage. Major media move as one "herd," following the leaders slavishly. National and international coverage differ very little from one newspaper to another within any given country.

The Bias Toward "Novelty" and "Sensationalism"

The "news" typically is constructed with a systematic bias in favor of reporting what is novel, bizarre, sensational, or odd. What happens every day — no matter how intrinsically important — is often sacri-ficed. But great social problems typically are embedded in day-to-day events that are repeated thousands of times. The individual events underlying them are often not dramatic or "odd" (but pathetically common).

On the one hand, if a large bank systematically overcharges millions of customers a small amount of money, it succeeds in stealing millions of dollars. But such a practice probably will not be considered news. If a solitary bank robber makes off with $10,000, on the other hand, that will make the news. If millions of children are bullied in schools every day, and suffer lifelong damage from that experience, that probably will not be considered news. But if a child has sex with another child at school, that will be considered news. If millions of children go to bed hungry every night all over the globe, that is not news. But if one school serves caviar during the school lunch, that is news. If women and children are sold everyday in an international slave trade, that is not news, but if a solitary teacher has a sexual relation with a student, that is news.

Critical Consumers of the News

Manipulating critical consumers of the news is difficult because:

- They study alternative perspectives and world views, learning how to interpret events from multiple viewpoints.

- They seek understanding and insight through multiple sources of thought and information, not simply those of the mass media.

- They learn how to identify the viewpoints embedded in news stories.

- They mentally rewrite (reconstruct) news stories through awareness of how stories would be told from multiple perspectives.

- They analyze news constructs in the same way they analyze other representations of reality (as some blend of fact and interpretation).

- They assess news stories for their clarity, accuracy, relevance, depth, breadth, and significance.

- They notice contradictions and inconsistencies in the news (often in the same story).

- They notice the agenda and interests served by a story.

- They notice the facts covered and the facts ignored.

- They notice what is represented as fact (that is in dispute).

- They notice questionable assumptions implicit in stories.

- They notice what is implied (but not openly stated).

- They notice what implications are ignored and what are emphasized.

- They notice which points of view are systematically put into a favorable light and which in an unfavorable light.

- They mentally correct stories reflecting bias toward the unusual, the dramatic, and the sensational by putting them into perspective or discounting them.

- They question the social conventions and taboos being used to define issues and problems.

Is It Possible for the News Media to Reform?

To provide their publics with non-biased writing, journalists around the world would have to, first, enter empathically into world views to which they are not at present sympathetic. They would have to imagine writing for audiences that hold views antithetical to the ones they hold. They would have to develop insights into their own sociocentrism. They would have to do the things that we have suggested are done by critical consumers of the news. The most significant problem is that, were they to do so, their articles would be perceived by their public as "biased" and "slanted," as "propaganda." These reporters would be seen as irresponsible, as allowing their personal point of view to bias their journalistic writings. Imagine Israeli journalists writing articles that present the Palestinian point of view sympathetically. Imagine Pakistani journalists writing articles that present the Indian point of view sympathetically.

> "The media world we inhabit is without exception a world of 'spin'"
>
> *The Wall Street Journal*
> May 7, 2004

The most basic point is this: Journalists do not determine the nature and demands of their job. They do not determine what their readers want or think or hate or fear. The nature and demands of their job are determined by the broader nature of societies themselves and the beliefs, values, and world views of its members. It is human nature to see the world, in the first instance, in egocentric and sociocentric terms. Most people are not interested in having their minds broadened. They want their present beliefs and values extolled and confirmed. Like football fans, they want the home team to win, and when it wins, to triumph gloriously. If it loses, they want to be told that the game wasn't important, or that the other side cheated, or that the officials were biased against them.

As long as the overwhelming mass of persons in the broader society are drawn to news articles that reinforce, and do not question, their fundamental views or passions, the economic imperatives will remain the same. The logic is parallel to that of reforming a nation's eating habits. As long as the mass of people want high-fat processed foods, the market will sell high-fat and processed foods to them. And as long as the mass of people want simplistic news articles that reinforce egocentric and sociocentric thinking, that present the world in sweeping terms of good and evil (with the reader's views and passions treated as good and those of the reader's conceived enemies as evil), the news media will generate such articles for them. The profit and ratings of news sources with their fingers on the pulse of their readers and viewers will continue to soar.

Is the Emergence of a "Critical Society" Possible?

In 1906, in a concluding chapter of his classic book, *Folkways*, William Graham Sumner raised the possibility of the development of "critical" societies, by which he meant societies that adopt critical thinking as an essential part of their way of life. Sumner recognized that critical thinking "is our only guarantee against delusion, deception, superstition, and misapprehension of ourselves and our earthly circumstances." He recognized education as "good just so far as it produces a well-developed critical faculty."

> "The critical habit of thought," he says, "if usual in a society, will pervade all its mores, because it is a way of taking up the problems of life. People educated in it cannot be stampeded...are slow to believe. They can hold things as possible or probable in all degrees, without certainty and without pain. They can wait for evidence and weigh evidence, uninfluenced by the emphasis or confidence with which assertions are made on one side or the other. They can resist appeals to their dearest prejudices and all kinds of cajolery. Education in the critical faculty is the only education of which it can be truly said that it makes good citizens."

No country or culture in the world routinely fosters education as perceived by Sumner. As things now stand, such education is the rare exception in any society. The detection of bias and propaganda in the news media is possible only for those who are willing to be diligent in pursuing news from multiple sources representing multiple alternative cultural and national standpoints. It is possible only for those who — in their reading and thinking and judging—are willing to swim against the tide.

Dominant and Dissenting Views: Finding Alternative Sources of Information

To find sources of information supporting the dominant views within a culture is not difficult. The problem for most of us is finding well-thought-through views that question the mainstream news. Thus, in the former Soviet Union, for example, it was hard to gain access to views that critiqued the Soviet line. It is always a minority of thinkers motivated to look beyond the dominant views who dig beneath the surface and bring forward what is unpleasant or painful to the majority. Critiques of a society within a society are typically hard to come by. Of course, the main point is that every society in the world today has mainstream and dissenting views. And it is important to recognize that we are not saying that dissenting views are correct and mainstream views incorrect. There are insights to be gained from all major conflicting world views. What is most important is to locate both mainstream and dissenting views (expressed in their most articulate and insightful forms). The ideal, for any given important issue, is access to a full range of views, as expressed by their most skilled and insightful defenders.

One faces two problems: 1) to locate a full range of views, and 2) to locate well-informed spokespersons for each major position in the spectrum.

Let us look at the United States. American mainstream views can be found in any of a large number of major American newspapers (the *New York Times,* the *Washington Post,* the *Baltimore Sun,* the *Boston Globe,* the *Chicago Tribune,* the *Cleveland Plain Dealer,* the *Los*

Angeles Times, the *Minneapolis Star Tribune,* the *Philadelphia Inquirer,* the *Sacramento Bee,* the *San Francisco Chronicle,* and so on). Similar lists of mainstream newspapers could be produced for every country in the world. Of course, there would be some overlap in viewpoints between mainstream newspapers from various nations and cultures, dependent on the extent to which they share religious views, economic interests, and political traditions.

Locating dissenting views within nations and cultures is more difficult, depending on the extent to which dissenters are forced to go "underground." The best general source for the views of important dissenters is through the scholarly magazines and presses of the world. In some cases, one can locate publications dealing with issues in greater depth than the mainstream news.

In the United States, for example, the *Nation* is one such publication. Founded in 1865, it has from its beginnings provided an outlet for intellectually dissenting points of view. Its contributors include: Nelson Algren, Hannah Arendt, W.H. Auden, James Baldwin, Willa Cather, Emily Dickinson, John Dos Passos, W.E.B. DuBois, Albert Einstein, Lawrence Ferlinghetti, Robert Frost, Carlos Fuentes, Emma Goldman, Langston Hughes, Henry James, Martin Luther King, Jr., D.H. Lawrence, Robert Lowell, Thomas Mann, H.L. Mencken, Arthur Miller, Pablo Neruda, Octavio Paz, Sylvia Plath, Ezra Pound, Bertrand Russell, Jean Paul Sartre, Upton Sinclair, Wallace Stevens, I.F. Stone, Gore Vidal, Kurt Vonnegut, Alice Walker, and William Butler Yeats. Clearly, this is a valuable source for non-mainstream points of view. In addition to providing a weekly magazine on controversial political and cultural issues, the *Nation* has also established a Digital Archive covering 6,500 issues. (see www.archive.thenation.com)

Of course, all sources of news and commentary should be read critically, carefully analyzed and assessed, and used as vehicles for intellectual independence, as sources for *part* of the truth, not as vehicles of THE TRUTH. The ideal is freedom from any one point of view or perspective.

Becoming an Independent Thinker

To detect bias and propaganda in the news media requires a commitment to thinking for oneself. The process of becoming an independent thinker is furthered significantly by reading the writings of famous dissenters, thinkers who in their day questioned the mainstream view. Each of the persons below critiqued the mainstream views of his or her day. Each thought outside the cultural box.

Tom Paine............................. (*Common Sense*, 1776)

William Lloyd Garrison .. (*The Journal of the Times and The Liberator*, 1831)

Wendell Phillips .... (*Speeches, Lectures, and Letters*, 1863)

Margaret Fuller .... (*Memoirs* [2 vols], 1852)

Henry David Thoreau.......... (*Essay on Civil Disobedience*, 1849)

Emma Goldman .... (*My Disillusionment with Russia*, 1923)

Henry George .... (*Social Problems*, 1883)

Thorstein Veblen... (*The Vested Interests and the Common Man*, 1919)

John Peter Altgeld..... (*Our Penal Machinery and Its Victims*, 1884)

Lincoln Steffens......... (*The Struggle for Self-Government*, 1906)

William Graham Sumner...................... (*Folkways*, 1906)

Gustavus Myers... (*History of the Great American Fortunes*, [2 vols], 1907)

Jose Ortega y Gasset............ (*The Revolt of the Masses*, 1932)

William J. Lederer.................... (*A Nation of Sheep*, 1961)

H.L. Mencken....................... (*Prejudices*, [6 vols], 1977)

Eric Hoffer .... (*The True Believer*, 1951))

Matthew Josephson .... (*The Robber Barons*, 1962)

Bertrand Russell..................... (*Unpopular Essays*, 1952)

C. Wright Mills........................ (*The Power Elite*, 1959)

Howard Zinn .... (*A People's History of the United States*, 1995)

Ralph Nader.................... (*The Ralph Nader Reader*, 2000)

Noam Chomsky................... (*Engineering Consent*, 1992)

Buried, Ignored, or
Underreported Stories

Of the millions of events that take place in the world on any given day, only a tiny percentage of them (a couple of hundred) are made into "news" stories (for a given culture). The stories selected typically confirm the dominant cultural viewpoint of the society. Stories that disconfirm the dominant cultural viewpoint are ignored, underreported, or "buried" (given little coverage and attention). Stories that are buried in the reporting of one culture, however, may be front-page news in the reporting of another.

This phenomenon is intensified when there is conflict between cultures. In this case, when the same event is covered, it is conceptualized very differently. For example, in wartime, each side tells the story of the conflict to its home audience in self-serving terms. Hence, though both sides commit atrocities, each side's media highlight only the atrocities of its enemy, while suppressing, denying, or minimizing its own. Each side conceptualizes itself as representing the forces of good (decency, justice, and so on) and its enemies as representing the forces of evil. The predictability of this self-serving function of mass media is highlighted in research into the mutual "image of the enemy":

> Enemy-images mirror each other — that is, each side attributes the same virtues to itself and the same vices to the enemy. "We" are trustworthy, peace-loving, honorable, and humanitarian; "they" are treacherous, warlike, and cruel. In surveys of Americans conducted in 1942, the first five adjectives chosen to characterize both Germans and Japanese (enemies) included warlike, and cruel, none of which appeared among the first five describing the Russians (allies); in 1966 all three had disappeared from American characterizations of the Germans and Japanese (allies), but now the Russians (no longer allies, although more rivals than enemies) were warlike and treacherous... The enemy-image acts like a distorting lens, which overemphasizes information that confirms it and filters out information that is incompatible with it. Thus the mass media play up incidents of an enemy's treachery or cruelty, and ignore examples of humanitarian or honorable behavior. (Jerome Frank, Chemtech, August 1982, p. 467)

In the pages that follow, we provide examples of stories that were buried, ignored, or underreported in the U.S. mass media. The buried stories were given low priority and minimal coverage in the major media. The ignored stories were found in dissenting alternative, non-mass media publications. In each case of an ignored story, pay special attention to how the story would disconfirm the dominant U.S. image of itself and/or of its role in the world, were it to be highlighted in the mass media. If buried or ignored stories actually were emphasized in the mass media, the public image of the United States as committed to freedom, justice, human rights, preservation of the earth's resources, international law, and democracy would be damaged.

Keep in mind that all countries' media project a favorable self-image of their own culture through a selection of what is and is not covered, what is given a positive spin, and what a negative spin. Our examples focus on what has been underreported or suppressed in the mass media in the United States, as we expect that the majority of our readers will be U.S. citizens. Our analysis could be paralleled in a similar study of the mass media's treatment of news *within any given country or culture.* Of course, the extent to which news is distorted within any country varies among countries and can be determined only through in-depth analysis, story by story.

Examples

The stories referred to in this section are a small selection of buried, underreported, or ignored stories in the mainstream media news. We have collected the "ignored" stories from sources outside the main stream of the mass media, sources that represent dissent largely unknown to the typical citizen within the culture. We have chosen to introduce each story in the form of the question the story raises. Readers whose views have been shaped principally by mass media sources would answer each question in the negative and would view the story as "biased."

1. **Do respected countries in the world consider the U.S. a danger to world peace?**
Source: *New York Times*, 2/3/03. "Arrogance may come back to haunt U.S.," editorial by Nicholas Kristof.

> "The European edition of Time magazine has been conducting a poll on its web site: 'Which country poses the greatest danger to world peace in 2003?' With 318,000 votes cast so far, the responses are: North Korea, 7 percent; Iraq, 8 percent; the United States, 84 percent."

Comment: We did not find this fact reported in the U.S. mass media, except as a passing comment in an editorial. The notion that the U.S. might be the country that poses the greatest danger to world peace is, of course, deeply incompatible with the U.S. self-image.

2. **To what extent is the U.S. responsible for atrocities of its allies?**
Source: *Newsweek*, Aug. 26, 2003. "The Death Convoy of Afghanistan" (mass media news article referring to events occurring in November 2002).

"In January, two investigators from the Boston-based Physicians for Human Rights had argued their way into Sheberghan prison [in Afghanistan]. What they saw shocked them. More than 3,000 Taliban prisoners – who had surrendered to the victorious Northern Alliance forces...were crammed, sick and starving, into a facility with room for only 800. The Northern Alliance commander of the prison acknowledged the charnel-house conditions, but pleaded that he had no money.... But stories of a deeper horror came from the prisoners themselves. However awful their conditions, they were the lucky ones. They were alive. Many hundreds of their comrades, they said, had been killed on the journey to Sheberghan from Konduz by being stuffed into sealed cargo containers and left to asphyxiate... Pentagon spokesmen have obfuscated when faced with questions on the subject. Officials across the administration did not respond to repeated requests by *Newsweek* for a detailed accounting of U.S. activities in the Konduz, Mazar-e Sharif and Sheberghan areas at the time in question, and Defense Department spokespersons have made statements that are false. According to Aziz ur Rahman Razekh, director of the Afghan Organization of Human Rights, "I can say with confidence that more than a thousand people died in the containers."

Comment: This story is exceptional in that it was *not* "buried" in *Newsweek*. However, it was suppressed or buried in virtually all of the other major news magazines and media sources, and to our knowledge, it has not been followed up in *Newsweek*.

3. Is the U.S. responsible for the deaths of more than half a million civilians in Iraq?

Source: *Mother Jones*, Nov/Dec. 2001. "The Betrayal of Basra," by Chuck Sudetic (*Mother Jones* is a dissenting, non-mass media source for news and commentary).

"For ten years the United States has been the staunchest advocate of maintaining a tight blockade on Iraq's access to foreign goods and its oil revenues. These restrictions have failed to loosen Saddam's grip on power. They have failed to force him to give up what is left of Iraq's chemical, biological, and nuclear weapons programs. What the sanctions have done, however, is kill... According to an estimate by Amatzia Baram, an Iraq analyst at the University of Haifa in Israel, between 1991 and 1997 half a million Iraqis died of malnutrition, preventable disease, lack of medicine, and other factors attributable to the sanctions; most were elderly people or children. The United Nations Children's Fund puts the death toll during the same period at more than 1 million of Iraq's 23 million people." According to this article, the Iraqi people "have come to see Saddam's worst enemy, the United States, as their enemy as well... Washington abandoned

[its] revolt against Saddam in 1991. Now [the] bitterness is tangible. And it will be ripe for exploitation by anti-American demagogues and terrorists for years after Saddam is gone." The article quotes an Iraqi now living in the U.S., "These people are not going to forget what has happened to them. In their eyes it is genocide. And people do not forget genocide."

4. Does the U.S. have a responsibility to live in accordance with the international treaties it signs?

Source: *Press Democrat*, Feb. 9, 2003. "Bush Seeks Exemption for Pesticide" (mass media news source).

According to this news source, in 1987, along with 182 other countries, the U.S. signed the Montreal Protocol, a treaty which calls for the elimination of chemicals that harm the ozone layer. But according to the article, U.S. farmers say there are no good alternatives to the use of methyl bromide, "a clear, odorless, gas that is injected into the soil every 18 months to kill worms, insects, rodents, and diseases.... The chemical was to be banned by 2005, in developed nations." The article states that the Bush administration therefore directed the EPA to seek an exemption for 16 uses of the chemical. The article quotes David Doniger, policy director of the climate center of the Natural Resources Defense Council, "We knew there were going to be some hard cases that needed extra time. But we never anticipated that the agribusiness industry would abuse the process and the Bush administration would kowtow to the growers and chemical companies this bad. It is thumbing its nose at the international treaty." According to this article, "bromide from methyl bromide is roughly 60 times more destructive to ozone on an atom-per-atom basis than the chlorine from CFCs" (chemicals once widely used in aerosols).

Commentary: This article was buried toward the back of a local news section.

5. Does the U.S. army operate a school that trains military officers in torture and murder techniques?

Source: *CounterPunch*, Feb.1-15, 2000. "New Army Plan for Torturers' School" (*CounterPunch* is a dissenting, non-mass media source of news and commentary).

According to *CounterPunch*, the School of the Americas, located in Fort Benning, Georgia, and run by the U.S. Army, is an institution "that has turned out 60,000 graduates, including many of the most vicious killers and torturers in the Latin American military... Year after year the U.S. Army has seethed at the growing campaign aimed at the School of the Americas... The annual protest rallies and civil disobedience outside Fort Benning have swelled in numbers, with 15,000 demonstrating last fall and 900 committing civil disobedience." The article goes on to say that because of these demonstrations, the Army recognizes the need to change its image. Thus the Secretary of the Army has drafted legislation that would replace the School of the Americas with the United States Military Institute for Hemispheric Security Cooperation. According to the article, "same place, new name." The article contends that the function of the new school will mirror that of the old one, "which is, as it has always been, the preparation of fresh cadres of military officers able and willing to carry out the proper custodial functions required of them by the American Empire."

6.   Is it humane for mentally ill inmates in U.S. prisons to be subjected to long-term solitary confinement?

Source: The *Nation* (March 3, 2003), "The SuperMax Solution," editorial by Regan Good (the *Nation* is a dissenting, non-mass media source for news and commentary).

According to this editorial, mentally ill inmates are increasingly confined to long-term solitary cells – known as supermax confinement. "Confined to their sells, alone, twenty-three hours a day, inmates eat, sleep, defecate, urinate, read and write (if they are able), watch TV or listen to the radio (if they are allowed) in the same 8-by-12 cell, often for years on end. The monotony, sensory deprivation, and mandated idleness…is especially torturous for inmates who have a serious mental illness." The article states that inmates must "earn" their way out of such confinement by correcting their behavior. But as Jean Maclean Snyder, an attorney representing mentally ill prisoners at Tamms prison, points out, many mental ill inmates can't "behave" in solitary confinement, by definition. "There is nothing to be good at, there is no behavior allowed." This article points out that, at any given moment, "there are about 25,000 people in long-term solitary confinement in the United States."

Commentary: On a related point, in 1998 the *New York Times* (Oct. 5) reported that Amnesty International was citing the United States for violating fundamental human rights within its own country, criticizing the U.S. criminal justice system for widespread cruelty and degrading practices. According to the *Times*, Pierre Sane, Secretary General of AI, said, "We felt it was ironic that the most powerful country in the world uses international human rights laws to criticize others but does not apply the same standards at home."

7.   To what extent has America been involved in crimes against humanity?

Source: *CovertAction Quarterly*, Winter 2001. "War Criminals, Real and Imagined," by Gregory Elich (*CovertAction Quarterly* is a dissenting news source). The following sections are summaries of information contained in this article, which cites 33 supporting references.

Indonesia: In 1965, a CIA-backed military coup toppled President Sukarno of Indonesia and brought to power General Suharto. Following the coup, between 500,000 and 1 million civilians were killed by the Suharto government. These civilians were trade unionists, peasants, ethnic Chinese, and members of the Indonesian Communist Party. During this time, the U.S. gave Suharto a list of thousands of communists within Indonesia it wanted killed and supplied him with covert military weapons. Once Suharto became acting president, the U.S. began to send economic aid to the country, and U.S. and Western European advisors helped chart economic policy. U.S. aid rose to $200 million by 1969, after Indonesia passed an investment law favorable to foreign companies. "In the years to come, New Order Indonesia would continue to imprison, torture, and execute several hundred thousand people."

Iran: In 1983, the CIA gave the Khomeini government a lengthy list of communists in the Tudeh Party, targeting these people as a threat, and hoping they would be arrested and executed. Eventually the entire party was eliminated by the Khomeini government, with deaths totaling 10,000 people. The Tudeh party leadership was tortured and forced to make false televised confessions. In 1989, again backed by the U.S. government, a special committee in Iran sentenced and executed 5,000 people from various political parties. Those executed were considered "leftists," and therefore a potential problem in a post-Khomeini government.

Cambodia: In 1975, the CIA-backed Khmer Rouge overthrew the government of Cambodia. Virtually the entire country was turned into a forced labor camp to implement a primitive agrarian economy. During the next four years, 2 million Cambodians died from starvation, disease and executions. Several hundred thousand were tortured and murdered. When the Khmer Rouge invaded Vietnam, an uprising of Cambodian people and Vietnam troops drove the Khmer Rouge from power. The U.S. backed the Khmer Rouge in launching guerrilla war against the new Cambodian socialist government. Through U.S. efforts, Vietnamese troops that were in Cambodia in support of the fledgling socialist government were driven out. Prince Norodom Sihanouk and Son Sann were forced into power, with U.S. insistence that Khmer Rouge play a major role in the new government. But since the people of Cambodia revolted against this idea, and the possibility of an international tribunal was becoming imminent, the Khmer Rouge offered to turn over its leader, Pol Pot to the U.S. government. The U.S. refused to take Pol Pot. Yet the U.S. managed to control the U.N. trials against the Khmer Rouge so that the role of the CIA in supporting the Khmer Rouge's egregious actions were never uncovered.

**8. Did the Bush administration threaten Mexico in order to get its U.N.
    vote for war on Iraq?**
Source: *Press Democrat,* March 10, 2003, "Let Them Hate as Long as They Fear,"
editorial by Paul Krugman (Mr. Krugman is a columnist for the *New York Times*).

According to this editorial, the Bush administration has threatened Mexico in
order to get its vote on the U.N. Security Council for an American war on Iraq.
New York Times columnist Paul Krugman states, "Last week the *Economist* quot-
ed an American Diplomat, who warned that if Mexico didn't vote for a U.S. res-
olution it could 'stir up feelings' against Mexicans in the United States. He com-
pared the situation to that of Japanese Americans who were interred after 1941,
and wondered whether Mexico 'wants to stir the fires of jingoism during the
war...' Then came President Bush's Monday interview with Copley News
Service. He alluded to the possibility of reprisals if Mexico didn't vote
America's way..." According to Krugman's column, Bush said that if Mexico
and other countries oppose the U.S., "There will be a certain sense of discipline." Krugman goes on to say, "These remarks went virtually unreported by
the ever-protective U.S. media, but they created a political firestorm in Mexico.
The White House has been frantically backpedaling, claiming that when Bush
talked of 'discipline,'he wasn't making a threat. But in the context of the rest of
the interview, it's clear that he was."

**9. Is the U.S. government violating international law and the U.N.
    Declaration of Human Rights by setting up assassination teams to kill
    persons they suspect are enemies?**
Source: *New York Times,* August 12, 2002, "Rumsfeld Weighs New Covert
Acts By Military Units."

"Defense Secretary Donald H. Rumsfeld is considering ways to expand broadly
the role of American Special Operations Forces in the global campaign against
terrorism, including sending them worldwide to capture or kill Al Qaeda leaders
far from the battlefields of Afghanistan, according to Pentagon and intelligence
officials... The discussion whether to give Special Operations Forces missions to
capture or kill individual Al Qaeda leaders may at some point conflict with the
executive order prohibiting assassinations."

Commentary: The U.N. Declaration of Human Rights, to which the U.S. is a
signatory, guarantees that anyone charged with a crime will have an opportunity to defend himself in a court of law. Those assassinated by American
Special Forces, however, will be killed based on the presumption or suspi-
cion of guilt. No neutral court of law will judge their evidence or provide
an opportunity for the accused to defend themselves. It is clear that the
U.S. would voice vehement objections if another country were to assassi-

nate Americans under parallel conditions. This contradiction certainly would be pointed out if this news item were reported in a Muslim newspaper.

10. **Is the United States "arrogant, self-indulgent, hypocritical, inattentive and unwilling or unable to engage in cross-cultural dialogue?"**
Source: *New York Times,* July 29, 2002, "Panel Urges U.S. to Revamp Efforts to Promote Image Abroad."

> "In a report to be released this week, the Council on Foreign Relations asserts that many countries, in particular predominantly Islamic ones, see the United States as "arrogant, self-indulgent, hypocritical, inattentive and unwilling or unable to engage in cross-cultural dialogue… The report acknowledges that American policies regarding Israel are a major impediment to improving the country's image in Muslim nations. But it chides the government for not doing more to…express concern about the 'suffering and grievances of the Palestinian people.' It also asserts that the Bush administration has weakened its standing abroad with 'misunderstood and/or misguided' policies that angered allies, including rejecting treaties to reduce global warming, ban antipersonnel land mines and create an International Criminal Court."

Commentary: Most mainstream media commentary on serious criticisms of the U.S. explains away the criticisms as based on jealousy and envy on the part of other countries. Most Americans (whose exposure to news is limited to mainstream mass media sources) believe that criticisms of U.S. policies are ill founded and without substance. Most versions of this report emphasized the need for the U.S. to do a better job presenting its image (as is indicated in the headline of this article), not in changing its policies.

11. **Is the United States (in threatening to attack Iraq) taking the law into its own hands and introducing chaos in international affairs?**
Source: Associated Press, Sept 3, 2002, "Nelson Mandela condemns U.S. threats to attack Iraq."

> "Johannesburg, South Africa-Nelson Mandela said Monday that he is "appalled" by U.S. threats to attack Iraq and warned that Washington is 'introducing chaos in international affairs'… 'We are really appalled by any country, whether a superpower or a small country, that goes outside the U.N. and attacks independent countries… No country should be allowed to take the law into [its] own hands. What they are saying is introducing chaos in international affairs, and we condemn that in the strongest terms.'"

Commentary: Since Nelson Mandela is a Nobel Peace Prize winner and an internationally renowned leader, this story was buried in most mainstream American media sources. It would be embarrassing to the U.S. government were his views to be given a major play in the U.S. mass media.

12. Did the United States try to block a U.N. anti-torture vote?

Source: Associated Press, July 25, 2002, "U.S. fails to block U.N. anti-torture vote."

"The United States failed to block a U.N. vote Wednesday on a plan to strengthen a treaty on torture, and was widely criticized by allies for trying to do so. The United States argued that the measure, known as a protocol, could pave the way for international and independent visits to U.S. prisons and to terror suspects being held by the U.S. military at Guantanamo Bay Naval Base in Cuba... The objective of the protocol is 'to establish a system of regular visits undertaken by independent and national bodies to places where people are deprived of their liberty, in order to prevent torture and other cruel, inhuman or degrading treatment or punishment... People were tortured or ill-treated by authorities in 111 countries last year, according to an Amnesty International report.'"

Commentary: This story was buried in most main stream American media sources, because it threatens the image of the U.S. as a country that stands for human rights and against such practices as the protocol condemns: "torture and other cruel, inhuman or degrading treatment and punishment."

13. Has the U.S. government tried to block the creation of an international war crimes tribunal and exempt America from its provisions?

Source: *Press Democrat*, March 12, 2003. "War Crimes Tribunal Sworn In"

"The World's first permanent war crimes tribunal was inaugurated Tuesday in the Netherlands, despite efforts by the Bush administration to hamper its creation and exempt America from its provisions. U.N. Secretary-General Kofi Annan presided as 18 international judges of the International Criminal Court took the oath of office at a ceremony before international dignitaries representing some of the 89 countries that back the court's establishment. Notably absent was an official representative of the United States."

Commentary: The explanation given by the U.S. State Department for its refusal to support a world court is, roughly, that any accusation of war crimes by a U.S. citizen brought before the court would be based on a "political" motivation. The unstated assumption seems to be that Americans are incapable of committing war crimes.

14. Did the U.S. try to defeat the World Health Organization sponsored treaty to ban cigarette ads worldwide?

Source: The *New York Times*, July 22, 2002. "W.H.O. Treaty Would Ban Cigarette Ads Worldwide."

Geneva: "Negotiators have drawn up a draft of an international treaty that would phase in bans on cigarette advertising and sports sponsorships by tobacco companies as part of the World Health Organization's campaign to curb smoking worldwide... The health agency says tobacco use is a serious threat to global health with more than 4 million people dying from smoking-related diseases each year... Anti-smoking campaigners have charged that the Bush administration has worked to undermine some of the toughest proposals, particularly concerning the ban on cigarette advertising. The United States has opposed any across-the-board ban on grounds that it would violate American free speech guarantees... The draft would require all nations that sign and ratify the treaty to draw up legislation 'for preventing and reducing tobacco consumption, nicotine addiction and exposure to tobacco smoke.' Subsidies for tobacco farming and manufacturing would be phased out, and eventually eliminated... The W.H.O has charged that the tobacco giants have been working behind the scenes to weaken the negotiating process..."

15. Does the U.S. share blame for the slaughter of 800,000 people in Rwanda in 1994, in the light of its knowledge of the slaughter and its deliberate decision to avoid getting involved to stop it?

Source: *Houston Chronicle*, August 22, 2001. "Papers Show U.S. Officials Knew of Rwanda Genocide."

"A set of newly declassified government documents shows that several senior U.S. officials were aware of the dimensions of the genocide in Rwanda in the spring of 1994, even as some officials sought ways to avoid getting involved. The 16 documents released Tuesday by the National Security Archive, a private research group at George Washington University provide new details of the deliberations within the Clinton administration from April through May of 1994 as the mass killings took place in Rwanda. By the end of June, an estimated 800,000 people had been killed by government-backed militias... Former President Clinton, during a March 1998 visit to Rwanda, expressed deep remorse about his administration's inaction and said Western governments must share responsibility for what happened... The documents also provide more details behind the U.S. government's decision to avoid calling the killings genocide... The officials worried that if the term genocide were used, Washington would be obliged to act because it was a signatory to an anti-genocide convention of 1948."

16. Is the hard-line criminalization of drug addiction leading to unconscionable injustices in sentencing and an unmanageable and overly costly prison system?

Source: *Newsweek*, February 12, 2001. "Special Report on Fighting Addiction."

"The aggregate consequences of addiction are staggering. Consider that the number of inmates in American prisons more than tripled over the last 20 years to nearly 2 million, with 60 to 70 percent testing positive for substance abuse on arrest. These inmates are the parents of 2.4 million children, all of whom are disproportionately likely to follow their parents to jail. According to the exponential math of a Brown University study, if the prison population were to continue growing at the current rate, by 2053 the United States would actually have more people in prison than out... George Pataki, once a major hard-liner, proposed cutting the minimum sentences for serious drug felons from 15 years to eight and giving judges more discretion. In reviewing the clemency process Pataki says he found 'dramatically unfair sentences — people sentenced to 15 years when their involvement was minimal.' But at the federal level, so-called mandatory minimum sentencing requirements are in no danger of being repealed any time soon. Spending priorities right now look pound foolish. The Center on Addiction and Substance Abuse released a study last week showing that states spend more than 13 percent of their total budgets just 'shoveling up' the wreckage of addiction — as much as they appropriate for higher education and 100 times what they spend on prevention and treatment. Another study by Rand Corp. shows that every dollar spent on treatment saves seven dollars in services. That's because even if addicts eventually relapse, they are clean during their time in treatment, saving millions in acute health-care costs and law enforcement."

17. Has the United States been a major supplier of biological agents to Iraq, agents used to make biological weapons?
Source: *New York Times*, March 16, 2003. "Iraq Links Germs For Weapons to U.S. and France."

"Iraq has identified a Virginia-based biological supply house and a French scientific institute as the sources of all the foreign germ samples that it used to create the biological weapons that are still believed to be in Iraq's arsenal, according to American officials and foreign diplomats who have reviewed Iraq's latest weapons declaration to the United Nations... The document shows that the American and French supply houses shipped 17 types of biological agents to Iraq in the 1980's that were used in the weapons programs. Those included anthrax and the bacteria needed to make botulinum toxin, among the most deadly poisons known... Gary Milhollin, director of the Wisconsin Project, an arms control research group, said that the biological supply houses should have realized that Iraq might use the germ samples to make weapons, especially since it was known then that Iraq used chemical weapons against Iranian troops in the Iran-Iraq war. 'If you know that the buying country is involved in a chemical weapons program, you have an obligation to ask some questions rather than just send it out,' Mr. Milhollin said."

18. Did the F.B.I. and the Justice Department deliberately mislead judges in justifying the "need" for electronic surveillance? Did the F.B.I and the Justice Department misuse information it obtained during such surveillance?

Source: *New York Times*, August 23, 2002. "Secret Court Says F.B.I. Aides Misled Judges in 75 Cases."

"The nation's secret intelligence court has identified more than 75 cases in which it says it was misled by the Federal Bureau of Investigation in documents in which the bureau attempted to justify its need for wire taps and other electronic surveillance, according to the first of the court's ruling to be released publicly. The opinion by the Foreign Intelligence Surveillance Court, which was issued in May but made public today by Congress, is stinging in its criticism of the F.B.I. and the Justice Department, which the court suggested had tried to defy the will of Congress by allowing intelligence material to be shared freely with criminal investigators... In essence, the court said that the F.B.I. and the Justice Department were violating the law by allowing information gathered from intelligence eavesdropping to be used freely in bringing criminal charges, without court review, and that criminal investigators were improperly directing the use of counterintelligence wiretaps...Gregory T. Nojeim, associate director of the national office of the American Civil Liberties Union in Washington, said the opinion was 'astounding' in demonstrating that the F.B.I. and the Justice Department tried an 'end run around the Fourth Amendment protections against reasonable searches.'"

19. Does the United States Government sanction the use of torture?"

Source: The *Nation*, March 31, 2003. "In Torture We Trust?" (article by Eyal Press).

"The recent capture of Al Qaeda leader Khalid Shaikh Mohammed is the latest indication that the taboo on torture has been broken. In the days after Mohammed's arrest, an unnamed official told the *Wall Street Journal* that U.S. interrogators may authorize 'a little bit of smacky-face' while questioning captives in the war on terrorism. Others proposed that the United States ship Mohammed off to a country where laxer rules apply. 'There's a reason why [Mohammed] isn't going to be near a place where he has Miranda rights or the equivalent,' a senior federal law enforcer told the *Journal*. 'You go to some other country that'll let us pistol-whip this guy.'... On December 26 of last year, the *Washington Post* published a front-page story detailing allegations of torture and inhumane treatment involving thousands of suspects apprehended since the

September 11 terrorist attacks. Al Qaeda captives held at overseas CIA interroga-
tions centers, which are completely off-limits to reporters, lawyers and outside
agencies, are routinely 'softened up' — that is beaten — by U.S. Army Special
Forces before interrogation, as well as thrown against walls, hooded, deprived of
sleep, bombarded with light and bound in painful positions with duct tape... The
same article reported that approximately 100 suspects have been transferred to
U.S. allies, including Saudi Arabia and Morocco, whose brutal torture methods
have been amply documented... 'We don't kick the [expletive] out of them,' one
official told the *Post*. 'We send them to other countries so they can kick the
[expletive] out of them'... Death certificates released for two Al Qaeda suspects
who died while in U.S. custody at the Bagram base in Afghanistan showed that
both were killed by 'blunt force injuries.' Other detainees told of being hung
from the ceiling in chains."

**20. Did the United States Government know that Iraq had destroyed its
chemical weapons and lie rather than admit their knowledge?**

Source: The *Nation*, April 7, 2003. "The Big Lie?" (article by Russ Baker).

"In its March 3 issue, *Newsweek* disclosed that the Bush Administration had
deliberately suppressed information exculpating Iraq — information from the
same reliable source previously cited by the Administration as confirming that
Iraq had developed weapons of mass destruction since the 1991 Gulf War. As
damning as this disclosure was, *Newsweek* chose to underplay it... Here's the
background: in the summer of 1995 Saddam's then son-in-law, Lieut. Gen.
Hussein Kamel, former minister of Iraq's military industry and the person in
charge of its nuclear/chemical/biological programs, defected and provided what
was deemed scrupulously accurate, detailed accounts of those weapons. Kamel's
information has been cited as central evidence and a key reason for attacking
Iraq. In his February 5 presentation to the U.N. Security Council, Secretary of
State Collin Powell said: 'It took years for Iraq to finally admit that it had produced four tons of the deadly nerve agent VX... This admission only came out
after inspectors collected documentation as a result of the defection of Hussein
Kamel, Saddam Hussein's late son-in-law.' But *Newsweek*'s John Barry revealed
that the Administration had excised a central component of Kamel's testimony
— that he had personal knowledge that Iraq had 'destroyed all its chemical and
biological weapons stocks and the missiles to deliver them.'... According to the
story, U.N. inspectors had reasons to hush up this revelation, as they were trying
to bluff Saddam into revealing more. But what is Powell's excuse for using only
half of Kamel's claim? And why did *Newsweek* and the rest of the American
media make so little of this major story? *Newsweek* chose to run a short, 500-
word item in its 'periscope' section rather than put the story on the cover or

make it the focal point of a longer article showing that the Bush Administration is rushing to war for no reason at all… Perhaps it's not surprising that other media failed to pick up on the Kamel story: The big papers and magazines hate to acknowledge they've been scooped by competitors… The Hussein Kamel revelation is probably the biggest Iraq story to get punted, but it isn't the only significant example… It's worth noting that British revelations that the National Security Agency spied on diplomats representing U.N. Security Council members during the Iraq deliberations got a small mention in the *Washington Post* and prompted no questions at Bush's press conference… Cumulatively, Barry's item on Kamel, the revelation that Colin Powell was citing a graduate student's thesis as British 'intelligence' and a new revelation that more British 'evidence' of Iraqi nuclear arms development cited by the Administration was (according to weapons inspectors themselves) fabricated suggest that a monstrous Big Lie is in process — an effort to construct falsified evidence and to trick this country and the world."

Every citizen in the world needs access to news sources and commentary that question the self-image maintained by the home culture through its own mass media. No culture lives up to the image it projects of itself. How inconsistent the "self-serving" image is with "reality" is a matter for the critically well-informed public to judge. In the case of the U.S., the stories above represent a small sampling of stories buried in the mass media coverage or largely unread in the dissenting non-mass media. Their portrayal of the U.S. is incompatible with the highly positive self-image in the preponderance of coverage in the mass media. For most U.S. consumers of the news, the self-image of the U.S. as defender of human rights, individual freedom, democratic values and social justice is unquestionably justified. What we need to remember, however, is that most consumers of the news media do not know how to bring forward "buried" information. They do not know how to read the news critically. Most have never seriously questioned their country's image. Therefore, they see no reason to seek out dissenting stories or to question highly nationalistic self-portraits. They cannot, therefore, exercise that higher patriotism that comes only through recognition of the vital need for constructive criticism; the patriotism that helps a country become more of what it has promised to be.

Using the Internet

The Internet can be used to locate both mainstream and dissenting views from virtually any country in the world. Below are three sources we located for non-mainstream viewpoints. As always, we do not offer sources as THE TRUTH but as aids in obtaining alternatives to the content of mainstream media news.

In some cases, particularly in countries where those with dissenting views are put in prison or killed, dissenting views must be sought from expatriates rather than from resident citizens. Amnesty International (www.amnesty.org) is a good source for discovering persons whose views are being forcibly suppressed. The organization publishes a quarterly news magazine focused on exposing the violations of human rights by nations all over the globe (*Amnesty Now*). (Visit www.aiusa.org)

A second example of the sort of important resource one can locate on the internet is "Statewatch." Statewatch serves as a watchdog organization and database whose goal is the monitoring of state and civil liberties in the European Union. To get a sense of its thoroughness, *Statewatch* has compiled 25,500 entries in its database since 1991, containing news features, sources, and reports. It publishes Statewatch, six times a year, in addition to pamphlets and reports. (Visit www.statewatch.org/)

A third example is *CovertAction Quarterly* (info@covertactionquarterly.org), whose goal is to document the involvement of intelligence agencies (such as the CIA, SDECE, MI-6, PIDE-DGS, SDC1, BOSS, MOSSAD and American, French, British, Portuguese, Italian, South African, and Israeli intelligence services) in actions violating human rights, and international and national laws. This publication documents acts typically "disowned" by the countries sponsoring them. Their sources are freelance investigative journalists, scholars, and former agents.

Another strategy is to search the Internet under descriptors such as "Japanese perspectives," "Asian perspectives," "Chinese perspectives," "African perspectives," "Central American perspectives," "South American perspectives" "Islamic Perspectives." This should help you locate a range of cultural and political standpoints.

Additional Alternative News Sources

Below are some non-mainstream scholarly sources of news, and background for the news. We assume that you will read these sources with the same criticality we are recommending for mainstream views. Once again, we do not offer these sources as THE TRUTH but, instead, as helpful non-mainstream viewpoints providing alternatives to the content of mainstream media news.

Harpers
www.harpers.org

The Progressive
www.progressive.org

Counter Punch
www.counterpunch.org

Common Dreams
www.commondreams.org

Indy Media Center
www.indymedia.org

The Nation
www.thenation.com/

Mother Jones
www.motherjones.com/

Free Speech T. V.
www.freespeach.org/

In These Times
www.inthesetimes.com/

Z Magazine
www.zmag.org/

AlterNet
www.alternet.org/

The Multinational Monitor
www.essential.org/monitor/

Dollars and Sense
www.dollarsandsense.org/

The Guardian
www.guardian.co.uk/

The Village Voice
www.villagevoice.com/

Project Censored
www.projectcensored.org/

Conclusion

Learning to detect media bias and propaganda in the national and world news is an art that takes extended time to develop. Yet it is also an art essential to intellectual responsibility, integrity, and freedom. This mini-guide presents a starting place for the development of intellectual analysis and assessment applied to news stories. As one develops in this art, one experiences a progressive shedding of layers of social indoctrination and ethnocentricity.

In the end, of course, each of us must decide for ourselves what to believe and how to act. We can do this critically or uncritically, rationally or irrationally, egocentrically or fair-mindedly. We can either tacitly accept our social conditioning and its accompanying ideology, or we can make a deliberative conscious choice to grow beyond that conditioning. The choice is ours. No one can legitimately make that choice for us. If we choose to go beyond our social conditioning and think for ourselves, we can become free persons and conscientious citizens.

An Abbreviated Glossary of
Critical Thinking Concepts and Terms

critical thinking: Self-directed, self-disciplined, self-monitored, and self-correc-
tive thinking. It presupposes assent to rigorous standards of excellence and mindful
command of their use. It entails effective communication and problem-solving
abilities and a commitment to overcome our native egocentrism and sociocentrism.
Everybody thinks; it is our nature to do so. But much of our thinking, left to itself,
is biased, distorted, partial, uninformed, or down-right prejudiced. Shoddy thinking
is costly, both in money and in quality of life. Excellence in thought through critical
thinking must be systematically cultivated. A well-cultivated critical thinker: raises
vital questions and problems, formulating them clearly and precisely; gathers and
assesses relevant information, using abstract ideas to interpret it effectively; comes
to well-reasoned conclusions and solutions, testing them against relevant criteria and
standards; thinks open-mindedly within alternative systems of thought, recognizing
and assessing, as need be, their assumptions, implications, and consequences; and
communicates effectively with others in figuring out solutions to complex problems.

cultural assumption: Unassessed (often implicit) belief adopted by virtue of
enculturation. Raised in a society, we unconsciously take on its point of view, values, beliefs, and practices. At the root of each of these are many assumptions. Not
knowing that we perceive, conceive, think, and experience within assumptions we
have taken in, we take ourselves to be perceiving "things as they are," not "things as
they appear from a cultural vantage point." Becoming aware of our cultural assumptions so that we critically examine them is a crucial dimension of critical thinking.

data: Facts, figures, and information from which conclusions can be inferred, or
upon which interpretations or theories can be based. As critical thinkers, we must
make certain to distinguish hard data from the inferences or conclusions we draw
from them.

egocentricity: A tendency to view everything in relationship to oneself; to con-
fuse immediate perception (how things seem) with reality; the tendency to be self-
centered or to consider only oneself and one's own interests; selfishness. One's
desires, values, and beliefs (seeming to be self-evidently correct, or superior to those
of others) are often uncritically used as the norm of all judgment and experience.
Egocentricity is one of the fundamental impediments to critical thinking. As one
learns to think critically, one learns to become more rational, and less egocentric.

ethnocentricity: A tendency to view one's own race or culture as privileged, based on the deep-seated belief that one's own group is superior to all others. Ethnocentrism is a form of egocentrism extended from the self to the group. Much uncritical or selfish critical thinking is either egocentric or ethnocentric in nature. (*Ethnocentrism* and *sociocentrism* are used synonymously, for the most part, though *sociocentricity* is broader, relating to any social group, including, for example, sociocentrism regarding one's profession.) The "cure" for ethnocentrism or sociocentrism is empathic thought within the perspective of opposing groups and cultures. Such empathic thought is rarely cultivated. Instead, many give mere lip service to tolerance, but privileging the beliefs, norms, and practices of their own culture. Critical thinkers do not assume that the groups to which they belong are inherently superior to other groups. Instead, they attempt to accurately critique every viewpoint, seeking to determine its strengths and weaknesses. Their loyalty to a country is based on the principles and ideals of the country and not on uncritical loyalty to person, party, or national traditions.

fair-mindedness: A cultivated disposition of mind that enables the thinker to treat all perspectives relevant to an issue in an objective manner. It implies having a consciousness of the need to treat all viewpoints alike, without reference to one's own feelings or selfish interests, or the feelings or selfish interests of one's friend's, community, or nation. It implies adherence to intellectual standards without reference to one's own advantage or the advantage of one's group.

human nature: The common qualities of all human beings. People have both a primary and a secondary nature. Our primary nature is spontaneous, egocentric, and strongly prone to the formation of irrational beliefs...the basis for our instinctual thought. People need no training to believe what they want to believe: what serves their immediate interests, what preserves their sense of personal comfort and righteousness, what minimizes their sense of inconsistency, and what presupposes their own correctness. People need no special training to believe what those around them believe: what their parents and friends believe, what is taught to them by religious and school authorities, what is repeated often by the media, and what is commonly believed in the nation in which they are raised. People need no training to think that those who disagree with them are wrong and probably prejudiced. People need no training to assume that their own most fundamental beliefs are self-evidently true or easily justified by evidence. People naturally and spontaneously identify with their own beliefs. They experience most disagreements as personal attacks. The resulting defensiveness interferes with their capacity to empathize with or enter into other points of view.

People need extensive and systematic practice to develop their secondary nature, their implicit capacity to function as rational persons. They need extensive and systematic practice to recognize the tendencies they have to form irrational beliefs. They need extensive practice to develop a dislike of inconsistency, an affinity for clarity, a passion to seek reasons and evidence and to be fair to points of view other than their own. People need extensive practice to recognize that they indeed have a point of view, that they live inferentially, that they do not have a direct pipeline to reality, that it is possible to have an overwhelming inner sense of the correctness of one's views and still be wrong.

intellectual autonomy: Having rational control of one's beliefs, values, and inferences. The ideal of critical thinking is to learn to think for oneself, to gain command over one's thought processes. Intellectual autonomy does not entail willfulness, stubbornness, or rebellion. It entails a commitment to analyzing and evaluating beliefs on the basis of reason and evidence, to question when it is rational to question, to believe when it is rational to believe, and to conform when it is rational to conform.

intellectual confidence or faith in reason: Assurance that in the long run one's own higher interests and those of humankind will best be served by giving the freest play to reason — by encouraging people to come to their own conclusions through a process of developing their own rational faculties; faith that (with proper encouragement and cultivation) people can learn to think for themselves, form rational viewpoints, draw reasonable conclusions, think coherently and logically, persuade each other by reason, and become reasonable, despite the deep-seated obstacles in the native character of the human mind and in society. Confidence in reason is developed through experiences in which one reasons one's way to insight, solves problems through reason, uses reason to persuade, is persuaded by reason. Confidence in reason is undermined when one is expected to accept beliefs on the sole basis of authority or social pressure.

intellectual courage: The willingness to face and fairly assess ideas, beliefs, or viewpoints to which we have not given a serious hearing, regardless of our strong negative reactions to them. This courage arises from the recognition that ideas considered dangerous or absurd are sometimes rationally justified (in whole or in part), and that conclusions or beliefs espoused by those around us or inculcated in us are sometimes false or misleading. To determine for ourselves which is which, we must not passively and uncritically "accept" what we have "learned." Intellectual courage comes into play here, because inevitably we will come to see some truth in certain ideas considered dangerous and absurd and some distortion or falsity in certain ideas strongly held in our social group. It takes courage to be true to our own thinking in such circumstances. Examining cherished beliefs is difficult, and the penalties for nonconformity are often severe.

intellectual empathy: Understanding the need to imaginatively put oneself in the place of others to genuinely understand them. We must recognize our egocentric tendency to identify truth with our immediate perceptions or longstanding beliefs. Intellectual empathy correlates with the ability to accurately reconstruct the viewpoints and reasoning of others and to reason from premises, assumptions, and ideas other than our own. This trait also requires that we remember occasions when we were wrong, despite an intense conviction that we were right, and consider that we might be similarly deceived in a case at hand.

intellectual humility: Awareness of the limits of one's knowledge, including sensitivity to circumstances in which one's native egocentrism is likely to function self-deceptively; sensitivity to bias and prejudice in, and limitations of, one's viewpoint. Intellectual humility is based on the recognition that no one should claim more than he or she actually knows. It does not imply spinelessness or submissiveness. It implies the lack of intellectual pretentiousness, boastfulness, or conceit, combined with insight into the strengths or weaknesses of the logical foundations of one's beliefs.

intellectual integrity: Recognition of the need to be true to one's own thinking, to be consistent in the intellectual standards one applies, to hold oneself to the same rigorous standards of evidence and proof to which one holds one's antagonists, to practice what one advocates for others, and to honestly admit discrepancies and inconsistencies in one's own thought and action. This trait develops best in a supportive atmosphere in which people feel secure and free enough to honestly acknowledge their inconsistencies, and can develop and share realistic ways of ameliorating them. It requires honest acknowledgment of the difficulties of achieving greater consistency.

intellectual discipline: The trait of thinking in accordance with intellectual standards, intellectual rigor, carefulness, order, conscious control. The undisciplined thinker cannot recognize when he or she comes to unwarranted conclusions, confuses ideas, fails to consider pertinent evidence, and so on. Thus, intellectual discipline is at the very heart of becoming a critical person. It takes discipline of mind to keep oneself focused on the intellectual task at hand, to locate and carefully assess needed evidence, to systematically analyze and address questions and problems, to hold one's thinking to intellectual standards such as clarity, precision, completeness, consistency, and so on.

intellectual perseverance: Willingness and consciousness of the need to pursue intellectual insights and truths despite difficulties, obstacles, and frustrations; firm adherence to rational principles despite irrational opposition of others;

a sense of the need to struggle with confusion and unsettled questions over an extended time to achieve deeper understanding or insight.

intellectual ˈsense of justice: Willingness and consciousness of the need to entertain all viewpoints sympathetically and to assess them with the same intellectual standards, without reference to one's own feelings or vested interests, or the feelings or vested interests of one's friends, community, or nation; implies adherence to intellectual standards without reference to one's own advantage or the advantage of one's group.

interpret/interpretation: To give one's own conception of, to place in the context of one's own experience, perspective, point of view, or philosophy. Interpretations should be distinguished from the facts, the evidence, the situation. (I may interpret someone's silence as an expression of hostility toward me. Such an interpretation may or may not be correct. I may have projected my patterns of motivation and behavior onto that person, or I may have accurately noticed this pattern in the other.) The best interpretations take the most evidence into account. Critical thinkers recognize their interpretations, distinguish them from evidence, consider alternative interpretations, and reconsider their interpretations in the light of new evidence.

multilogical (multidimensional) problems: Problems that can be analyzed and approached from more than one, often from conflicting, points of view or frames of reference. For example, many ecological problems have a variety of dimensions: historical, social, economic, biological, chemical, moral, political, and so on. A person comfortable thinking through multilogical problems is comfortable thinking within multiple perspectives, in engaging in dialogical and dialectical thinking, in practicing intellectual empathy, in thinking across disciplines and domains.

multilogical thinking: Thinking that sympathetically enters, considers, and reasons within multiple points of view.

national bias: Prejudice in favor of one's country, it's beliefs, traditions, practices, image, and world view; a form of sociocentrism or ethnocentrism. It is natural, if not inevitable, for people to be favorably disposed toward the beliefs, traditions, practices, and world view within which they were raised. Unfortunately, this favorable inclination commonly becomes a form of prejudice: a more or less rigid, irrational ego-identification that significantly distorts one's view of one's own nation and the world at large. It is manifested in a tendency to mindlessly take the side of one's own government, to uncritically accept governmental accounts of the nature of disputes with other nations, to uncritically exaggerate the virtues of one's own nation while playing down the virtues of "enemy" nations. National bias is reflected in the press and media coverage of every nation of the world. Events are included or excluded according to what appears significant within the dominant world view of the nation, and are shaped into stories to validate that view. Though constructed to fit into a particular view of the world, the stories in the news are presented as neutral, objective accounts, and uncritically accepted as such because people tend to uncritically assume that their own view of things is the way things really are. To become responsible, critically thinking citizens and fair-minded people, students must practice identifying national bias in the news and in their texts, and to broaden their perspective beyond that of uncritical nationalism.

point of view (perspective): Human thought is relational and selective. It is impossible to understand any person, event, or phenomenon from every vantage point simultaneously. Our purposes often control how we see things. Critical thinking requires that this fact be taken into account when analyzing and assessing thinking. This is not to say that human thought is incapable of truth and objectivity, but only that human truth, objectivity, and insight is almost always limited and partial, not total and absolute. By "reasoning within a point of view," then, we mean that inevitably our thinking has some comprehensive focus or orientation. Our thinking is focused ON something FROM some angle. We can change either what we are focused on or the angle of our focus. We often give names to the angle from which we are thinking about something. For example, we could look at something politically or scientifically, poetically or philosophically. We might look at something conservatively or liberally, religiously or secularly. We might look at something from a cultural or a financial perspective, or both. Once we understand how someone is approaching a question or topic (what their comprehensive perspective is), we are usually much better able to understand the logic of his or her thinking as an organized whole.

prejudice: A judgment, belief, opinion, point of view — favorable or unfavorable — formed before the facts are known, resistant to evidence and reason, or in disregard of facts that contradict it. Self-announced prejudice is rare. Prejudice almost always exists in obscured, rationalized, socially validated, functional forms. It enables people to sleep peacefully at night even while flagrantly abusing the rights of others. It enables people to get more of what they want, or to get it more easily. It often is sanctioned with a superabundance of pomp and self-righteousness. Unless we recognize these powerful tendencies toward selfish thought in our social institutions, even in what appear to be lofty actions and moralistic rhetoric, we will not face squarely the problem of prejudice in human thought and action. Uncritical and selfishly critical thought are often prejudiced.

self-deception: Deceiving oneself about one's true motivations, character, identity. One possible definition of the human species is "The Self-Deceiving Animal." Self-deception is a fundamental problem in human life and the cause of much human suffering. A fundamental goal of critical thinking is to overcome self-deception through self-reflection.

social contradiction: An inconsistency between what a society preaches and what it practices. In every society there is some degree of inconsistency between its image of itself and its actual character. Social contradiction typically correlates with human self-deception on the social or cultural level. Critical thinking is essential for the recognition of inconsistencies, and recognition is essential for reform and eventual integrity.

sociocentricity: The assumption that one's own social group is inherently and self-evidently superior to all others. When a group or society sees itself as superior, and so considers its views as correct or as the only reasonable or justifiable views, and all its actions as justified, it has a tendency to presuppose this superiority in all of its thinking and, thus, to think closed-mindedly. All dissent and doubt are considered disloyal and rejected without consideration. Few people recognize the sociocentric nature of much of their thought.

vested interest: 1) Involvement in promoting personal advantage, usually at the expense of others, 2) people functioning as a group to pursue collective selfish goals and exerting influences that enables them to profit at the expense of others. Many groups that lobby Congress do so to gain money, power, and advantage for themselves by provisions in law that specially favor them. The term *vested interest* classically contrasts with the term *public interest*. A group that lobbies Congress in the public interest is not seeking to gain special advantage for a comparative few but, rather, protection for virtually all or the large majority. Preserving the quality of the air is a public interest. Building cheaper cars by including fewer safety features is a vested interest (it makes more money for car manufacturers).

The Thinker's Guide Library

The Thinker's Guide
To
Strategic Thinking
25 Weeks to Better Thinking and Better Living
First Steps to Becoming a Critical Thinker
By Dr. Linda Elder and Dr. Richard Paul
The Foundation for Critical Thinking

The Thinker's Guide
to
Critical and Creative Thinking
by
Dr. Linda Elder and Dr. Richard Paul
Based on Critical Thinking Concepts & Principles
The Foundation for Critical Thinking

The Thinker's Guide to
How to Read a Paragraph
and beyond
The Art of Close Reading
How to Read a Text Worth Reading and Take Ownership of Its Important Ideas
By Dr. Richard Paul and Dr. Linda Elder
Based on Critical Thinking Concepts & Tools
The Foundation for Critical Thinking

The Miniature Guide
to
Critical Thinking
CONCEPTS & TOOLS
by
Dr. Richard Paul and Dr. Linda Elder
The Foundation for Critical Thinking
www.criticalthinking.org
707-878-9100
cct@criticalthinking.org

The Miniature Guide
For Those Who Teach
On
Practical Ways To Promote
Active & Cooperative Learning
by
Dr. Wesley Hiler and Dr. Richard Paul
Based on Critical Thinking Concepts & Principles
Note: This guide is best followed up by the guide: "How to Improve Student Learning"

The Miniature Guide
to
Understanding the Foundations of
Ethical Reasoning
by
Dr. Linda Elder and Dr. Richard Paul
Based on Critical Thinking Concepts & Principles
The Foundation for Critical Thinking

The Miniature Guide
to
Taking Charge of
The Human Mind
by
Dr. Linda Elder and Dr. Richard Paul
Based on Critical Thinking Concepts & Principles
The Foundation for Critical Thinking

A Miniature Guide
For Students and Faculty
To
Scientific Thinking
By Dr. Richard Paul and Dr. Linda Elder
Based on Critical Thinking Concepts & Principles
The Foundation for Critical Thinking

A Miniature Guide
For Those Who Teach
On
How to Improve Student Learning
30 PRACTICAL IDEAS
by
Dr. Richard Paul and Dr. Linda Elder
Based on Critical Thinking Concepts & Principles
A Companion To:
A Miniature Guide on How to Study and Learn,
A Miniature Guide to Active and Cooperative Learning,
A Miniature Guide to Critical Thinking

The Miniature Guide
to
The Art of
Asking Essential Questions
by
Dr. Linda Elder and Dr. Richard Paul
Based on Critical Thinking Concepts and Socratic Principles
The Foundation for Critical Thinking

A Miniature Guide
For Students
On
How to Study & Learn
a discipline
using critical thinking concepts & tools
By Richard Paul and Linda Elder
This is a companion to
"The Miniature Guide to Critical Thinking" by Paul & Elder

A Miniature Guide
for Students and Faculty
To
Analytic Thinking
How To Take Thinking Apart
And What To Look For When You Do
The Elements of Thinking and
The Standards They Must Meet
By Dr. Linda Elder and Dr. Richard Paul
Based on Critical Thinking Concepts & Principles
The Foundation for Critical Thinking

The Thinker's Guide to
How to Write a Paragraph
The Art of Substantive Writing
How to say something worth saying
about something worth saying something about
By Dr. Richard Paul and Dr. Linda Elder
Based on Critical Thinking Concepts & Tools
Companion to How to Read a Paragraph
The Foundation for Critical Thinking

The Miniature Guide
For Conscientious Citizens
on
How to Detect Media Bias and Propaganda
In National and World News
by
Dr. Richard Paul and Dr. Linda Elder
Based on Critical Thinking Concepts & Tools
The Foundation for Critical Thinking

The Miniature Guide
to
Critical Thinking for Children
(to help you think better and better)
By Fairminded Fran (And Linda Elder)